# The Princess De

Madame de La Fayette

Alpha Editions

This edition published in 2024

ISBN 9789362092359

Design and Setting By

**Alpha Editions**

www.alphaedis.com

Email - info@alphaedis.com

As per information held with us this book is in Public Domain.
This book is a reproduction of an important historical work.
Alpha Editions uses the best technology to reproduce historical work
in the same manner it was first published to preserve its original nature.
Any marks or number seen are left intentionally to preserve.

# The Princess de Montpensier

This story was written by Madame de Lafayette and published anonymously in 1662. It is set in a period almost 100 years previously during the sanguinary wars of the counter-reformation, when the Catholic rulers of Europe, with the encouragement of the Papacy, were bent on extirpating the followers of the creeds of Luther and Calvin. I am not qualified to embark on a historical analysis, and shall do no more than say that many of the persons who are involved in the tale actually existed, and the events referred to actually took place. The weak and vicious King and his malign and unscrupulous mother are real enough, as is a Duc de Montpensier, a Prince of the Blood, who achieved some notoriety for the cruelty with which he treated any Huguenots who fell into his hands, and for the leadership he gave to the assassins during the atrocious massacre of St. Bartholomew's day.

He was married and had progeny, but the woman to whom he was married was not the heroine of this romance, who is a fictional character, as is the Comte de Chabannes.

The Duc de Guise of the period whose father had been killed fighting against the Protestants, did marry the Princess de Portein, but this was for political reasons and not to satisfy the wishes of a Princess de Montpensier.

It will be noticed, I think, that women were traded in marriage with little or no regard to their personal emotions, and no doubt, as has been remarked by others, marriages without love encouraged love outside marriage. Whatever the reality, the literary conventions of the time seem to have dictated that we should be treated only to ardent glances, fervent declarations, swoonings and courtly gestures; we are not led even to the bedroom door, let alone the amorous couch. I wonder, however, if the reader might not think that this little tale written more than three hundred years ago contains the elements of many of the romantic novels and soap operas which have followed it.

At one level it is a cautionary tale about the consequences of marital infidelity; at another it is a story of a woman betrayed, treated as a pretty bauble for the gratification of men, and cast aside when she has served her purpose, or a butterfly trapped in a net woven by uncaring fate. Her end is rather too contrived for modern taste, but, even today, characters who are about to be written out of the plot in soap operas are sometimes smitten by mysterious and fatal disorders of the brain.

The unfortunate Comte de Chabannes is the archetypical "decent chap," the faithful but rejected swain who sacrifices himself for the welfare of his beloved without expectation of reward. In the hands of another writer, with some modification, he could have provided a happy ending in the "Mills and Boon" tradition.

This translation is not a schoolroom exercise, for although I have not altered the story, I have altered the exact way in which it is told in the original, with the aim of making it more acceptable to the modern reader. All translation must involve paraphrase, for what sounds well in one language may sound ridiculous if translated literally into another, and it is for the translator to decide how far this process may be carried. Whether I have succeeded in my task, only the reader can say.

## Mézières

It was while the civil war of religion was tearing France apart that the only daughter of the Marquis of Mézières, a very considerable heiress, both because of her wealth and the illustrious house of Anjou from which she was descended, was promised in marriage to the Duc de Maine, the younger brother of the Duc de Guise.

The marriage was delayed because of the youth of this heiress, but the elder of the brothers, the Duc de Guise, who saw much of her, and who saw also the burgeoning of what was to become a great beauty, fell in love with her and was loved in return. They concealed their feelings with great care; the Duc de Guise, who had not yet become as ambitious as he was to become later, wanted desperately to marry her, but fear of angering his uncle, the Cardinal de Lorraine, who had taken the place of his dead father, prevented him from making any declaration.

This was how the matter stood when the ruling house of Bourbon, who could not bear to see any benefit accruing to that of de Guise, decided to step in and reap the profit themselves by marrying this heiress to the Prince de Montpensier.

This project was pursued with such vigour that the parents of Mlle. de Mézières, despite the promises given to the Cardinal de Lorraine, resolved to give her in marriage to the young Prince. The house of de Guise was much displeased at this, but the Duc himself was overcome by grief, and regarded this as an insupportable affront. In spite of warnings from his uncles, the Cardinal and the Duc de Aumale—who did not wish to stand in the way of something which they could not prevent—he expressed himself with so much violence, even in the presence of the Prince de Montpensier, that a mutual enmity arose between them which lasted all their lives.

Mlle. de Mézières, urged by her parents to marry the Prince, realised that it was impossible for her to marry the Duc de Guise, and that if she married his brother, the Duc de Maine, she would be in the dangerous position of having as a brother-in-law a man whom she wished was her husband; so she agreed finally to marry the Prince and begged the Duc de Guise not to continue to place any obstacle in the way.

The marriage having taken place, the Prince de Montpensier took her off to his estate of Champigny, which was where Princes of his family usually lived, in order to remove her from Paris, where it seemed that an outbreak of fighting was imminent: this great city being under threat of siege by a Huguenot army led by the Prince de Condé, who had once more declared war on the King.

The Prince de Montpensier had, when a very young man, formed a close friendship with the Comte de Chabannes, a man considerably older than himself and of exemplary character. The Comte in turn had been so much influenced by the esteem and friendship of the Prince that he had broken off influential connections which he had with the Prince de Condé, and had declared for the Catholics; a change of sides which, having no other foundation, was regarded with suspicion: so much so that the Queen Mother, Catherine de Medici, on the declaration of war by the Huguenots, proposed to have him imprisoned. The Prince de Montpensier prevented this and carried him away to Champigny when he went there with his wife. The Comte being a very pleasant, amiable man soon gained the approbation of the Princess and before long she regarded him with as much friendship and confidence as did her husband. Chabannes, for his part, observed with admiration the beauty, sense and modesty of the young Princess, and used what influence he had to instill in her thoughts and behaviour suited to her elevated position; so that under his guidance she became one of the most accomplished women of her time.

The Prince having gone back to the Court, where he was needed owing to the continuation of the war, the Comte lived alone with the Princess and continued to treat her with the respect due to her rank and position. The Princess took him so far into her confidence as to tell him of the feelings she had once had for the Duc de Guise, but she intimated that there remained only enough of this emotion to prevent her heart from straying elsewhere and that this remnant, together with her wifely virtue made it impossible for her to respond, except with a rebuff, to any possible suitor.

The Comte who recognised her sincerity and who saw in her a character wholly opposed to flirtation and gallantry, did not doubt the truth of her words; but nevertheless he was unable to resist all the charms which he saw daily so close to him. He fell deeply in love with the Princess, in spite of the shame he felt at allowing himself to be overcome by this illicit passion. However although not master of his heart, he was master of his actions; the change in his emotions did not show at all in his behaviour, and no one suspected him. He took, for a whole year, scrupulous care to hide his feelings from the Princess and believed that he would always be able to do so.

Love, however, had the same effect on him as it does on everyone, he longed to speak of it, and after all the struggles which are usually made on such occasions, he dared to tell her of his devotion. He had been prepared to weather the storm of reproach which this might arouse, but he was greeted with a calm and a coolness which was a thousand times worse than the outburst which he had expected. She did not take the trouble to be angry. She pointed out in a few words the difference in their rank and ages, she reminded him of what she had previously said about her attitude to suitors and above all to the duty he owed to the confidence and friendship of the Prince her husband. The Comte was overwhelmed by shame and distress. She tried to console him by assuring him that she would forget entirely what he had just said to her and would always look on him as her best friend; assurances which were small consolation to the Comte as one might imagine. He felt the disdain which was implicit in all that the Princess had said, and seeing her the next day with her customary untroubled looks redoubled his misery.

The Princess continued to show him the same goodwill as before and even discussed her former attachment to the Duc de Guise, saying that she was pleased that his increasing fame showed that he was worthy of the affection she had once had for him. These demonstrations of confidence, which were once so dear to the Comte, he now found insupportable, but he did not dare say as much to the Princess, though he did sometimes remind her of what he had so rashly confessed to her.

After an absence of two years, peace having been declared, the Prince de Montpensier returned to his wife, his renown enhanced by his behaviour at the siege of Paris and the battle of St. Denis. He was surprised to find the beauty of the Princess blooming in such perfection, and being of a naturally jealous disposition he was a little put out of humour by the realisation that this beauty would be evident to others beside himself. He was delighted to see once more the Comte, for whom his affection was in no way diminished. He asked him for confidential details about his wife's character and temperament, for she was almost a stranger to him because of the little time during which they had lived together. The Comte, with the utmost sincerity, as if he himself were not enamoured, told the Prince everything he knew about the Princess which would encourage her husband's love of her, and he also suggested to Madame de Montpensier all the measures she might take to win the heart and respect of her spouse. The Comte's devotion led him to think of nothing but what would increase the happiness and well-being of the Princess and to forget without difficulty the interest which lovers usually have in stirring up trouble between the objects of their affection and their marital partners.

The peace was only short-lived. War soon broke out again by reason of a plot by the King to arrest the Prince de Condé and Admiral Chatillon at Noyers. As a result of the military preparations the Prince de Montpensier was forced to leave his wife and report for duty. Chabannes, who had been restored to the Queen's favour, went with him. It was not without much sorrow that he left the Princess, while she, for her part, was distressed to think of the perils to which the war might expose her husband.

The leaders of the Huguenots retired to La Rochelle. They held Poitou and Saintongne; the war flared up again and the King assembled all his troops. His brother, the Duc d'Anjou, who later became Henri III, distinguished himself by his deeds in various actions, amongst others the battle of Jarnac, in which the Prince de Condé was killed. It was during this fighting that the Duc de Guise began to play a more important part and to display some of the great qualities which had been expected of him. The Prince de Montpensier, who hated him, not only as a personal enemy but as an enemy of his family, the Bourbons, took no pleasure in his successes nor in the friendliness shown toward him by the Duc d'Anjou.

After the two armies had tired themselves out in a series of minor actions, by common consent they were stood down for a time. The Duc d'Anjou stayed at Loches to restore to order all the places which had been attacked. The Duc de Guise stayed with him and the Prince de Montpensier, accompanied by the Comte de Chabannes, went back to Champigny, which was not far away.

The Duc d'Anjou frequently went to inspect places where fortifications were being constructed. One day when he was returning to Loches by a route which his staff did not know well, the Duc de Guise, who claimed to know the way, went to the head of the party to act as guide, but after a time he became lost and arrived at the bank of a small river which he did not recognise. The Duc d'Anjou had a few words to say to him for leading them astray, but while they were held up there they saw a little boat floating on the river, in which—the river not being very wide— they could see the figures of three or four women, one of whom, very pretty and sumptuously dressed, was watching with interest the activities of two men who were fishing nearby.

This spectacle created something of a sensation amongst the Princes and their suite. It seemed to them like an episode from a romance. Some declared that it was fate that had led the Duc de Guise to bring them there to see this lovely lady, and that they should now pay court to her. The Duc d'Anjou maintained that it was he who should be her suitor.

To push the matter a bit further, they made one of the horsemen go into the river as far as he could and shout to the lady that it was the Duc d'Anjou who wished to cross to the other bank and who begged the lady to take him in her boat. The lady, who was of course the Princess de Montpensier, hearing that it was the Duc d'Anjou, and having no doubt when she saw the size of his suite that it was indeed him, took her boat over to the bank where he was. His fine figure made him easily distinguishable from the others; she, however, distinguished even more easily the figure of the Duc de Guise. This sight disturbed her and caused her to blush a little which made her seem to the Princes to have an almost supernatural beauty.

The Duc de Guise recognised her immediately in spite of the changes which had taken place in her appearance in the three years since he had last seen her. He told the Duc d'Anjou who she was and the Duc was at first embarrassed at the liberty he had taken, but then, struck by the Princess's beauty, he decided to venture a little further, and after a thousand excuses and a thousand compliments he invented a serious matter which required his presence on the opposite bank, and accepted the offer which she made of a passage in her boat. He got in, accompanied only by the Duc de Guise, giving orders to his suite to cross the river elsewhere and to join him at Champigny, which Madame de Montpensier told him was not more than two leagues from there.

As soon as they were in the boat the Duc d'Anjou asked to what they owed this so pleasant encounter. Madame de Montpensier replied that having left Champigny with the Prince her husband with the intention of following the hunt, she had become tired and having reached the river bank she had gone out in the boat to watch the landing of a salmon which had been caught in a net. The Duc de Guise did not take part in this conversation, but he was conscious of the re-awakening of all the emotions which the Princess had once aroused in him, and thought to himself that he would have difficulty in escaping from this meeting without falling once more under her spell.

They arrived shortly at the bank where they found the Princess's horses and her attendants who had been waiting for her. The two noblemen helped her onto her horse where she sat with the greatest elegance. During their journey back to Champigny they talked agreeably about a number of subjects and her companions were no less charmed by her conversation than they had been by her beauty. They offered her a number of compliments to which she replied with becoming modesty, but a little more coolly to those from M. de Guise, for she wished to maintain a distance which would prevent him from founding any expectations on the feelings she had once had towards him.

When they arrived at the outer courtyard of Champigny they encountered the Prince de Montpensier, who had just returned from the hunt. He was greatly astonished to see two men in the company of his wife, and he was even more astonished when, on coming closer, he saw that these were the Duc d'Anjou and the Duc de Guise. The hatred which he bore for the latter, combined with his naturally jealous disposition made him find the sight of these two Princes with his wife, without knowing how they came to be there or why they had come to his house, so disagreeable that he was unable to conceal his annoyance. He, however, adroitly put this down to a fear that he could not receive so mighty a Prince as the King's brother in a style befitting his rank. The Comte de Chabannes was even more upset at seeing the Duc de Guise and Madame de Montpensier together than was her husband, it seemed to him a most evil chance which had brought the two of them together again, an augury which foretold disturbing sequels to follow this new beginning.

In the evening Madame de Montpensier acted as hostess with the same grace with which she did everything. In fact she pleased her guests a little too much. The Duc d'Anjou who was very handsome and very much a ladies man, could not see a prize so much worth winning without wishing ardently to make it his own. He had a touch of the same sickness as the Duc de Guise, and continuing to invent important reasons, he stayed for two days at Champigny, without being obliged to do so by anything but the charms of Madame de Montpensier, for her husband did not make any noticeable effort to detain him. The Duc de Guise did not leave without making it clear to Madame de Momtpensier that he felt towards her as he had done in the past. As nobody knew of this former relationship he said to her several times, in front of everybody, that his affections were in no way changed. A remark which only she understood.

Both he and the Duc d'Anjou left Champigny with regret. For a long time they went along in silence; but at last it occurred to the Duc d'Anjou that the reflections which occupied his thoughts might be echoed in the mind of the Duc de Guise, and he asked him brusquely if he was thinking about the beauties of Madame de Montpensier. This blunt question combined with what he had already observed of the Prince's behaviour made the Duc realise that he had a rival from whom it was essential that his own love for the Princess should be concealed. In order to allay all suspicion he answered with a laugh that the Prince himself had seemed so preoccupied with the thoughts which he was accused of having that he had deemed it inadvisable to interrupt him; the beauty of Madame de Montpensier was, he said, nothing new to him, he had been used to discounting its effect since the days when she was destined to be his sister-in-law, but he saw that not everyone was so little dazzled. The Duc d'Anjou admitted that he had never seen anyone to compare with this young Princess and that he was well aware that the vision might be dangerous if he was exposed to it too often. He tried to get the Duc de Guise to confess that he felt the same, but the Duc would admit to nothing.

On their return to Loches they often recalled with pleasure the events which had led to their meeting with the Princess de Montpensier, a subject which did not give rise to the same pleasure at Champigny. The Prince de Montpensier was dissatisfied with all that had happened without being able to say precisely why. He found fault with his wife for being in the boat. He considered that she had welcomed the Princes too readily; and what displeased him most was that he had noticed the attention paid to her by the Duc de Guise. This had provoked in him a furious bout of jealousy in which he recalled the anger displayed by the Duc at the prospect of his marriage, which caused him to suspect that even at that time the Duc was in love with his wife. The Comte de Chabannes as usual made every effort to act as peacemaker, hoping in this way to show the Princess that his devotion to her was sincere and disinterested. He could not resist asking her what effect the sight of the Duc de Guise had produced. She replied that she had been somewhat upset and embarrassed at the memory of the feelings she had once displayed to him; she found him more handsome than he had been then and it had seemed to her that he wished to persuade her that he still loved her, but she assured the Comte that nothing would shake her determination not to become involved in any intrigue. The Comte was happy to hear of this resolve, but he was far from being sure about the Duc de Guise. He earnestly warned the Princess of the danger of a return to the previous situation should she have any change of heart, though when he spoke of his devotion she adopted her invariable attitude of looking on him as her closest friend but in no way a possible suitor.

The armies were once more called up; all the Princes returned to their posts and the Prince de Montpensier decided that his wife should come with him to Paris so as to be further from the area where it was expected that fighting would take place. The Huguenots besieged Poitiers. The Duc de Guise went there to organise the defence and, while there, enhanced his reputation by his conduct. The Duc d'Anjou suffered from some illness, and left the army either on account of the severity of this or because he wanted to return to the comfort and security of Paris, where the presence of the Princess de Montpensier was not the least of the attractions. The command of the army was taken over by the Prince de Montpensier, and shortly after this, a peace having been arranged, the Court assembled in Paris. Here the beauty of the Princess eclipsed that of all her rivals. She charmed everyone by her looks and personality. The Duc d'Anjou did not abandon the sentiments she had inspired in him at Champigny, he took great care to make her aware of this by all sorts of delicate considerations, being careful at the same time not to make his attentions too obvious for fear of arousing the jealousy of her husband. The Duc de Guise was now fervently in love with her, but wishing, for a variety of reasons, to keep this secret, he resolved to tell her so privately and avoid any preliminaries which, as always, would give rise to talk and exposure. One day when he was in the Queen's apartments where there were very few people, the Queen having left to discuss affairs of state with Cardinal de Lorraine, the Princess de Montpensier arrived. He decided to take this opportunity to speak to her, and going up to her he said, "Although it may surprise and displease you, I want you to know that I have always felt for you that emotion which you once knew so well, and that its power has been so greatly increased by seeing you again that neither your disapproval, the hatred of your husband, nor the rivalry of the first Prince in the kingdom can in the least diminish it. It would perhaps have been more tactful to have let you become aware of this by my behaviour rather than by my words, but my behaviour would have been evident to others as well as to yourself and I wanted you alone to know of my love for you."

The Princess was so surprised and thrown into confusion by this speech that she could not think of an answer, then, just when she had collected her wits and begun to reply, the Prince de Montpensier entered the room. The Princess's face displayed her agitation, and her embarrassment was compounded by the sight of her husband, to such an extent that he was left in no doubt about what the Duc de Guise had been saying to her. Fortunately at that moment the Queen re-entered the room and the Duc de Guise moved away to avoid the jealous Prince.

That evening the Princess found her husband in the worst temper imaginable. He berated her with the utmost violence and forbade her ever to speak to the Duc de Guise again. She retired to her room very sad and much preoccupied with the events of the day. She saw the Duc the next day amid the company around the Queen, but he did not come near her and left soon after she did, indicating that he had no interest in remaining if she was not there. Not a day passed without her receiving a thousand covert marks of the Duc's passion though he did not attempt to speak to her unless he was sure that they could be seen by nobody.

Convinced of the Duc's sincerity, the Princess, in spite of the resolution she had made at Champigny, began to feel in the depths of her heart something of what she had felt in the past.

The Duc d'Anjou for his part, omitted nothing which could demonstrate his devotion in all the places where he could meet her. In the Queen his mother's apartments he followed her about continually, completely ignoring his sister who was very fond of him. It was at around this time that it became evident that this sister, who later became the Queen of Navarre, had a liking for the Duc de Guise, and another thing that became evident was a cooling of the friendship between that Duc and the Duc d'Anjou. The rumour linking the name of the Royal Princess with that of the Duc de Guise disturbed the Princess de Montpensier to a degree which surprised her, and made her realise that she was more interested in the Duc than she had supposed.

Now it so happened that her father-in-law, M. de Montpensier, married a sister of the Duc de Guise, and the princess was bound to meet the Duc frequently in the various places where the marriage celebrations required their presence. She was greatly offended that a man who was widely believed to be in love with "Madame", the King's sister, should dare to make advances to her; she was not only offended but distressed at having deceived herself.

One day, when they met at his sister's house, being a little separated from the rest, the Duc was tempted to speak to her, but she interrupted him sharply saying angrily "I do not understand how, on the basis of a weakness which one had at the age of thirteen, you have the audacity to make amorous proposals to a person like me, particularly when, in the view of the whole Court, you are interested in someone else." The Duc who was intelligent as well as being much in love, understood the emotion which underlay the Princess's words. He answered her most respectfully, "I confess, Madame, that it was wrong of me not to reject the possible honour of becoming the King's brother-in-law, rather than allow you to suspect for a moment that I could desire any heart but yours; but if you will be patient enough to hear me I am sure I can fully justify my behaviour." The Princess made no reply, but she did not go away and the Duc, seeing that she was prepared to listen to him, told her that although he had made no effort to attract the attention of Madame, she had nevertheless honoured him with her interest: as he was not enamoured of her he had responded very coolly to this honour until she gave him to believe that she might marry him. The realisation of the grandeur to which such a marriage would raise him had obliged him to take a little more trouble. This situation had aroused the suspicions of the King and the Duc d'Anjou, but the opposition of neither of them would have any effect on his course of action, however, if this displeased her he would abandon all such notions and never think of them again.

This sacrifice which the Duc was prepared to make caused the Princess to forget all the anger she had shown. She changed the subject and began to speak of the indiscretion displayed by Madame in making the first advances and of the considerable advantages which he would gain if he married her. In the end, without saying anything kind to the Duc de Guise, she made him recall a thousand things he had found so pleasing in Mlle. de Mézières. Although they had not had private conversation for a long time, they found themselves attuned to one another, and their thoughts went along a track which they both had travelled in the past. At the end of this agreeable meeting the Duc was left in a state of considerable happiness, and the Princess was not a little moved to think that he truly loved her. However, in the privacy of her room she became ashamed of the ease with which she had accepted the Duc's excuses and reflected on the trouble into which she might be plunged if she engaged in something she had always regarded with distaste and on the frightening misery which a jealous husband might inflict on her. These thoughts made her adopt new resolves, but they disappeared the next day on the sight of the Duc de Guise.

The new alliance between their families gave the Duc many opportunities to speak to her. He gave her an exact account of all that passed between Madame and himself. He had difficulty in allaying the jealousy to which the beauty of Madame gave rise and any number of promises failed to reassure her. This jealousy enabled the Princess to defend the remains of her heart against the advances of the Duc, who already had won the greater part of it.

The marriage of the King to the daughter of the Emperor Maximilian filled the Court with fêtes and celebrations. The King put on a ballet in which Madame and all the princesses were to dance; among them only the Princess de Montpensier could rival Madame in beauty. The Duc d'Anjou and four others were to make an appearance as Moors; their costumes would all be identical, as was usual in this sort of performance. On the first occasion on which the ballet was presented, the Duc de Guise, before the dance began and before he had donned his mask, said a few words to the Princess as he went past her. She saw clearly that the Prince her husband had noticed this, which made her feel uneasy. A little later, seeing the Duc d'Anjou in his mask and Moorish costume, who was coming to speak to her, she mistook him for the Duc de Guise and said to him "Do not have eyes for anyone but Madame this evening: I shall not be in the least jealous. I am ordering you. I am being watched. Do not come near me again." As soon as she had said this she moved away.

The Duc d'Anjou stood there thunderstruck. He saw that he had a successful rival: the reference to Madame made it obvious that this was the Duc de Guise, and left him in no doubt that his sister was to play second fiddle to the Princess de Montpensier. Jealousy, frustration and rage joining to the dislike which he already had for the Duc roused him to a violent fury; and he would have given there and then some bloody mark of his temper had not that dissimulation which came naturally to him prevented him from attacking the Duc de Guise in the present circumstances. He did not, however, refrain from the pleasure of disclosing his knowledge of this secret affair. He approached the Duc de Guise as they left the salon where they had been dancing and said to him "To presume to raise your eyes towards my sister, as well as stealing the affection of the woman I love is altogether too much. The presence of the King prevents me from taking any action just now, but remember that the loss of your life may be, one day, the least thing with which I shall punish your impertinence."

The pride of the Duc de Guise was not accustomed to submit tamely to such threats, but he was unable to reply because at that moment the King called both of them to his side. He did not forget, however, and tried all his life to exact revenge.

From that evening the Duc d'Anjou endeavoured in all sorts of ways to turn the King against the Duc de Guise. He persuaded the King that Madame would never agree to her proposed marriage to the King of Navarre as long as the Duc de Guise was allowed to have any contact with her; and that it was unacceptable that a subject, for his own vain purposes, should place an obstacle in the way of what could bring peace to France. The King already disliked the Duc de Guise and this speech inflamed his dislike so much that the next day when the Duc presented himself to join the ball at the Queen's apartments, he stood in the doorway and asked him brusquely where he was going. The Duc, without showing any surprise answered that he had come to offer his most humble services, to which the King replied that he had no need of any services which the Duc might provide, and turned away without any other acknowledgement. The Duc was not deterred from entering the room, his feelings incensed both against the King and the Duc d'Anjou. His natural pride led him, as an act of defiance, to pay more attention to Madame than usual, and what the Duc d'Anjou had told him prevented him from looking in the direction of the Princess de Montpensier.

The Duc d'Anjou watched both of them with close attention. The Princess's expression, in spite of herself, showed some chagrin when the Duc de Guise spoke with Madame. The Duc d'Anjou who realised from what she had said to him, when she mistook him for the Duc de Guise, that she was jealous, hoped to cause trouble. He drew close to her and said,

"It is in your interest and not in mine that I must tell you that the Duc de Guise does not deserve the choice you have made of him in preference to me, a choice which you cannot deny and of which I am well aware. He is deceiving you, Madame, and betraying you for my sister as he betrayed her for you. He is a man moved only by ambition, but since he has the good fortune to please you, that is enough; I shall not attempt to stand in the way of a felicity which without doubt I merit more than he. It would be undignified for me to persist in trying to gain the heart which is already possessed by another. It is bad enough to have attracted only your indifference and I would not like to have this replaced by dislike by wearying you with endless protestations of unwelcome devotion."

The Duc d'Anjou who was genuinely touched by love and sadness, was hardly able to complete this speech, and although he had begun in a spirit of spite and vengeance, he was so overcome when he thought of the Princess's beauty and of what he was losing by giving up all hope of being her lover, that without waiting for her reply he left the ball, saying that he felt unwell, and went home to nurse his grief.

The Princess de Montpensier stayed there, upset and worried as one might imagine. To see her reputation and her secret in the hands of a suitor whom she had rejected and to learn from him that she was being deceived by her lover were not things which would put her in the right frame of mind for a place dedicated to enjoyment; she had, however, to remain where she was and later go to supper in the company of the Duchess de Montpensier, her mother-in-law.

The Duc de Guise who had followed them to his sister's house, was dying to tell her what the Duc d'Anjou had said the day before, but to his astonishment when he did have the opportunity to speak to her, he was overwhelmed by reproaches which were tumbled out in such angry profusion that all he could gather was that he was accused of infidelity and treachery. Dismayed at finding himself in this unhappy situation when he had hoped for consolation, and being so much in love with the Princess that he could not bear to be unsure if he was loved in return, he took a sudden decision. "I shall lay your doubts at rest." He said. "I am going to do what all the royal power could not make me do. It will cost me my fortune but that is of little account if it makes you happy."

He went straight from his sister's house to that of his uncle, the cardinal. He convinced him that having fallen into the King's disfavour, it was essential that it should be made quite clear that he would not marry Madame, so he asked for his marriage to be arranged with the Princess de Portien, a matter which had previously been discussed. The news of this was soon all over Paris and gave rise to much surprise. The princess de

Montpensier was both happy and sad. Glad to see the power she had over the Duc, and sorry that she had caused him to abandon something so advantageous as marriage to Madame. The Duc who hoped that love would compensate him for his material loss, pressed the Princess to give him a private audience so that he could clear up the unjust accusations which she had made. He obtained this when she found herself at his sister's house at a time when his sister was not there and she was able to speak to him alone. The Duc took the opportunity to throw himself at her feet and describe all that he had suffered because of her suspicions, and though the Princess was unable to forget what the Duc d'Anjou had said to her, the behaviour of the Duc de Guise did much to reassure her. She told him exactly why she believed he had betrayed her which was because the Duc d'Anjou knew what he could only have learned from him. The Duc did not know how to defend himself and was as puzzled as she to guess what could have given away their secret: at last, while the Princess was remonstrating with him for giving up the idea of the advantageous marriage with Madame and rushing into that with the Princess de Portien, she said to him that he could have been certain that she would not be jealous since on the day of the ball she herself had told him to have eyes only for Madame. The Duc said that she might have intended to do so but that she certainly had not. She maintained that she had, and in the end they reached the correct conclusion that she herself, deceived by the resemblance of the costumes, had told the Duc d'Anjou what she accused the Duc de Guise of telling him. The Duc de Guise who had almost entirely returned to favour, did so completely as a result of this conversation. The Princess could not refuse her heart to a man who had possessed it in the past and had just made such a sacrifice to please her. She consented to accept his declaration and permitted him to believe that she was not unmoved by his passion. The arrival of the Duchess, her mother-in-law, put an end to this tête-à-tête, and prevented the Duc from demonstrating his transports of joy.

Some time later, the Court having gone to Blois, the marriage between the King of Navarre and Madame was celebrated. The Duc de Guise who wanted nothing more than the love of the Princess de Montpensier, enjoyed a ceremony which in other circumstances would have overwhelmed him with disappointment.

The Duc was not able to conceal his love so well that the Prince de Montpensier did not suspect that something was going on, and being consumed by jealousy he ordered his wife to go to Champigny. This order was a great shock to her, but she had to obey: she found a way to say goodbye to the Duc de Guise privately but she found herself in great difficulty when it came to a means of providing a method whereby he could write to her. After much thought she decided to make use of the Comte de

Chabannes, whom she always looked on as a friend without considering that he was in love with her. The Duc de Guise, who knew of the close friendship between the Comte and the Prince de Montpensier, was at first amazed at her choice of the Comte as a go-between, but she assured him of the Comte's fidelity with such conviction that he was eventually satisfied. He parted from her with all the unhappiness which such a separation can cause.

The Comte de Chabannes, who had been ill in Paris while the Princess was at Blois, learning that she was going to Champigny arranged to meet her on the road and go with her. She greeted him with a thousand expressions of friendship and displayed an extraordinary impatience to talk to him in private, which at first delighted him. Judge his dismay when he found that this impatience was only to tell him that she was loved passionately by the Duc de Guise, a love which she returned. He was so distressed that he was unable to reply. The Princess, who was engrossed by her infatuation, took no notice of his silence. She began to tell him all the least details of the events, and how she and the Duc had agreed that he should be the means by which they could exchange letters. The thought that the woman he loved expected him to be of assistance to his rival, and made the proposal as if it was a thing he would find agreeable was bitterly hurtful, but he was so much in control of himself that he hid all his feelings from her and expressed only surprise at the change in her attitude. He hoped that this change which removed even the faintest hope from him would at the same time change his feelings, but he found the Princess so charming, her natural beauty having been enhanced by a certain grace which she had acquired at Court that he felt that he loved her more than ever. This remarkable devotion produced a remarkable effect. He agreed to carry his rival's letters to his beloved.

The Princess was very despondent at the absence of the Duc de Guise, and could hope for solace only from his letters. She continually tormented the Comte de Chabannes to know if he had received any and almost blamed him for not having delivered one sooner. At last some arrived, brought by a gentleman in the Duc's service, which he took to her immediately so as not to delay her pleasure for a moment longer than necessary. The Princess was delighted to have them and tortured the poor Comte by reading them to him, as well as her tender and loving reply. He took this reply to the waiting courier even more sadly than he had made the delivery. He consoled himself a little by the reflection that the Princess would realise what he was doing for her and would show some recognition. Finding, however, that she daily treated him with less consideration, owing to the anxieties which preoccupied her, he took the liberty of begging her to think a little of the suffering she was causing him. The Princess who had nothing in her head but the Duc de Guise, was so irritated by this approach that she treated the Comte much worse than she had done on the first occasion when he had declared his love for her. Although his devotion and patience had stood so many trials, this was too much. He left the Princess and went to live with a friend who had a house in the neighbourhood, from where he wrote to her with all the bitterness that her behaviour had provoked and bid her an eternal adieu.

The Princess began to repent having dealt so harshly with a man over whom she had so much influence, and being unwilling to lose him, not only on account of their past friendship, but also because of his vital role in the conduct of her affair, she sent a message to him to say that she wished to speak to him one more time and that afterwards she would leave him free to do as he pleased. One is very vulnerable when one is in love. The Comte came back, and in less than an hour the beauty of the Princess, her charm and a few kind words made him more submissive than ever, and he even gave her some letters from the Duc de Guise which he had just received.

At this time there was a scheme afoot in the Court to attract there all the leaders of the Huguenots, with the secret aim of including them in the horrible massacre of St. Bartholomew's day. As part of this attempt to lull them into a false sense of security, the King dismissed from his presence all the princes of the houses of Bourbon and de Guise. The Prince de Montpensier returned to Champigny, to the utter dismay of his wife, the Duc de Guise went to the home of his uncle, the Cardinal de Lorraine.

Love and idleness induced in him such a violent desire to see the Princess de Montpensier that without considering the risks to her and to himself he made some excuse to travel and leaving his suite in a small town he took with him only the gentleman who had already made several trips to Champigny, and went there by post-chaise. As he knew no one whom he could approach but the Comte de Chabannes, he had the gentleman write a note requesting a meeting at a certain spot. The Comte, believing that this was solely for the purpose of receiving letters from the Duc de Guise went there, but was most surprised to see the Duc himself and equally dismayed. The Duc, full of his own plans, took no more notice of the Comte's dismay than had the Princess of his silence when she told him of her amour. He described his passion in florid terms and claimed that he would infallibly die if the Princess could not be persuaded to see him. The Comte replied coldly that he would tell the Princess all that the Duc wanted to convey and would return with her response. He then went back to Champigny with his own emotions in such a turmoil that he hardly knew what he was doing. He thought of sending the Duc away without saying anything to the Princess, but the faithfulness with which he had promised to serve her soon put an end to that idea. He arrived without knowing what he should do, and finding that the Prince was out hunting, he went straight to the Princess's apartment. She saw that he was distressed and dismissed her women in order to find out what troubled him. He told her, as calmly as he could, that the Duc de Guise was a league distant and that he wanted passionately to see her. The Princess gave a cry at this news and her confusion was almost as great as that of the Comte. At first she was full of joy at the thought of seeing the man she loved so tenderly, but when she considered how much this was against her principles, and that she could not see her lover without introducing him into her home during the night and without her husband's knowledge, she found herself in the utmost difficulty. The Comte awaited her reply as if it were a matter of life or death. Realising that her silence indicated her uncertainty, he took the liberty of presenting to her all the perils to which she would be exposed by such a meeting, and wishing to make it clear that he was not doing this in his own interest, he said that if, in spite of all that he had said she was determined to see the Duc, rather than see her seek for aid from helpers less faithful than himself, he would bring the Duc to her. "Yes Madame," he said, "I shall go and find the Duc and bring him to your apartment, for it is too dangerous to leave him for long where he is."

"But how can this be done?" interrupted the Princess.

"Ha! Madame," cried the Comte, "It is then decided, since you speak only of the method. I shall lead him through the park; only order one of your maids whom you can trust to lower, exactly at midnight, the little drawbridge which leads from your antechamber to the flower garden and leave the rest to me." Having said this he rose and without waiting for any further comment from the Princess, he left, remounted his horse and went to look for the Duc de Guise, who was waiting for him with the greatest impatience.

The Princess remained in such a state of confusion that it was some time before she came to her senses. Her first thought was to send someone after the Comte to tell him not to bring the Duc, but she could not bring herself to do so. She then thought that failing this she had only not to have the drawbridge lowered, and she believed that she would continue with this resolve, but when the hour of the assignation drew near she was no longer able to resist the desire to see the lover whom she longed for, and she gave instructions to one of her women on the method by which the Duc was to be introduced into her apartment.

Meanwhile the Duc and the Comte were approaching Champigny, but in very differing frames of mind. The Duc was full of joy and all the happiness of expectation. The Comte was in a mood of despair and anger, which tempted him at times to run his sword through his rival. They at last reached the park, where they left their horses in the care of the Duc's squire, and passing through a gap in the wall they came to the flower garden. The Comte had always retained some hope that the Princess would come to her senses and resolve not to see the Duc, but when he saw that the drawbridge was lowered he realised that his hope was in vain. He was tempted to take some desperate measure, but he was aware that any noise would be heard by the Prince de Montpensier whose rooms looked out onto the same flower-garden, and that all the subsequent disorder would fall on the head of the one he loved most. He calmed himself and led the Duc to the presence of the Princess. Although the Princess signaled that she would like him to stay in the room during the interview, he was unwilling to do so, and retired to a little passage which ran alongside the Princess's apartment, a prey to the saddest thoughts which could afflict a disappointed lover.

Now, although they had made very little noise while crossing the bridge, the Prince de Montpensier was awake and heard it. He made one of his servants get up and go to see what it was. The servant put his head out of the window and in the darkness he could make out that the drawbridge was lowered. He told his master who then ordered him to go into the park and find out what was going on. A moment later he got up himself, being disturbed by what he thought he had heard, that is, footsteps on the bridge leading to his wife's quarters.

As he was going towards the little passage where the Comte was waiting, the Princess who was somewhat embarrassed at being alone with the Duc de Guise, asked the latter several times to come into the room. He refused to do so and as she continued to press him and as he was furiously angry he answered her so loudly that he was heard by the Prince de Montpensier, but so indistinctly that the Prince heard only a man's voice without being able to recognise it as that of the Comte.

These events would have infuriated a character more placid and less jealous than the Prince de Montpensier. He hurled himself against the door, calling for it to be opened, and cruelly surprising the Princess, the Duc de Guise and the Comte de Chabannes. This last, hearing the Prince's voice, saw immediately that it was impossible to prevent him from believing that there was someone in his wife's room, and that he was in such a state that if he found that it was the Duc de Guise he might kill him before the eyes of the Princess and that even her life might be at risk. He decided, in an act of extraordinary generosity, to sacrifice himself to save a successful rival and an ungrateful mistress.

While the Prince was battering on the door, he went to the Duc, who had no idea what to do, put him in the care of the woman who had arranged his entry by the bridge and told her to show him the way out. Scarcely had he left when the Prince having broken down the door entered the room like a man possessed. However when he saw only the Comte de Chabannes, motionless, leaning on a table with a look of infinite sadness on his face, he stopped short. The astonishment of finding his best friend alone at night in his wife's room deprived him of speech. The Princess had collapsed onto some cushions and never perhaps has fate put three people in a more unhappy position. At last the Prince made an attempt to make sense of the chaos before his eyes. He addressed the Comte in a tone of voice which still had some friendliness, "What is this I see?" he said, "Is it possible that a man I love so dearly has chosen among all other women to seduce my wife? And you, Madame," he said, turning to his wife, "Was it not enough to deprive me of your love and my honour without depriving me of the one man who could have consoled me in such circumstances? Answer me, one of you," he said to them, "And explain this affair, which I cannot believe is what it seems." The Princess was incapable of replying and the Comte opened his mouth once or twice but was unable to speak.

"You see me as a criminal," he said at last. "And unworthy of the friendship you have shown me; but the situation is not what you may think it is. I am more unhappy than you and more despairing. I do not know how to tell you more than that. My death would avenge you, and if you were to kill me now you would be doing me a favour." These words, spoken with an air of the deepest sorrow, and in a manner which declared his innocence instead of enlightening the Prince confirmed him in the view that something mysterious was going on which he did not understand. His unhappiness was increased by this uncertainty. "Kill me yourself," he said. "Or give me some explanation of your words for I can understand nothing. You owe it to my friendship, you owe it to my restraint, for anyone but me would have already taken your life to avenge such an affront."

"The appearances are wholly misleading," interrupted the Comte.

"Ah! It is too much. I must be avenged and clear things up later," said the Prince, advancing towards the Comte like a man carried away by rage. The Princess, fearing bloodshed, (which was not possible as her husband did not have a sword) placed herself between the two of them and fell fainting at her husband's feet. The Prince was even more affected by this than he was by the calmness of the Comte when he confronted him, and as if he could no longer bear the sight of those two people who had caused him such distress, he turned away and fell on his wife's bed, overcome by grief. The Comte de Chabannes, filled with remorse at having abused the friendship of which he had had so many marks, and believing that he could never atone for what he had done, left the room abruptly and passing through the Princess's apartment where he found all the doors open, he went down to the courtyard. He had a horse brought to him and rode off into the country led only by his feelings of hopelessness. The Prince de Montpensier, seeing that his wife did not recover from her faint, left her to her women and retired to his own quarters greatly disturbed.

The Duc de Guise having got out of the park, hardly knowing what he was doing being in such a state of turmoil, put several leagues between himself and Champigny, but could go no further without news of the Princess. He stopped in the forest and sent his squire to find out from the Comte de Chabannes what had happened. The squire found no trace of Chabannes but was told by others that the Princess was seriously ill. The Duc's inquietude was increased by what the squire had told him, but as he could do nothing he was constrained to go back to his uncle's in order not to raise suspicions by too long an absence.

The Duc's squire had been correct when he said that the Princess was seriously ill, for as soon as her women had put her to bed she was seized by a violent fever with horrible phantasies, so that by the second day her life was despaired of. The Prince pretended that he himself was ill so that no one should be surprised that he did not visit his wife's room. The order which he received to return to the Court, to which all the Catholic princes were being recalled in preparation for the massacre of the Huguenots, relieved him of his embarrassment. He went off to Paris without knowing what he had to hope or fear about his wife's illness. He had hardly arrived there when the assault on the Huguenots was signalised by the attack on admiral de Chatillon. Two days later came the disgraceful massacre, now so well known throughout Europe.

The poor Comte de Chabannes who had gone to hide himself away in one of the outer suburbs of Paris to abandon himself to his misery was caught up in the ruin of the Huguenots. The people to whose house he had retired, having recognised him, and having recalled that he had once been suspected of being of that persuasion, murdered him on the same night which was fatal to so many people. The next day the Prince de Montpensier, who was in that area on duty, passed along the street where the body of the Comte lay. He was at first shocked by this pitiful sight and, recalling his past friendship, was grieved; but then the memory of the offence, which he believed the Comte had committed, made him feel pleased that he had been avenged by the hand of chance.

The Duc de Guise who had used the opportunity of the massacre to take ample revenge for the death of his father, gradually took less and less interest in the condition of the Princess of Montpensier; and having met the Marquise de Noirmoutier, a woman of wit and beauty, and one who promised more than the Princess de Montpensier, he attached himself to her, an attachment which lasted a lifetime.

The Princess's illness reached a crisis and then began to remit. She recovered her senses and was somewhat relieved by the absence of her husband. She was expected to live, but her health recovered very slowly because of her low spirits, which were further depressed by the realisation that she had received no news of the Duc de Guise during all her illness. She asked her women if they had not seen anyone, if they had not had any letters, and finding that there had been nothing, she saw herself as the most wretched of women, one who had risked all for a man who had abandoned her. A fresh blow was the news of the death of the Comte de Chabannes, which her husband made sure she heard about as soon as possible. The ingratitude of the Duc de Guise made her feel even more deeply the loss of a man whose fidelity she knew so well. These disappointments weighed heavily upon her and reduced her to a state as serious as that from which she had recently recovered. Madame de Noirmoutier was a woman who took as much care to publicise her affairs as others do to conceal them. Her relations with the Duc de Guise were so open that, even though far away and ill, the Princess heard so much about it that she was left in no doubt. This was the final straw. She had lost the regard of her husband, the heart of her lover, and the most loyal of her friends. She took to her bed, and died not long after in the flower of her youth. She was one of the loveliest of women and could have been one of the happiest if she had not strayed so far from the path of prudence and virtue.

Milton Keynes UK
Ingram Content Group UK Ltd.
UKHW030627061024
449204UK00004B/238